T0292997

VALUE-ADDED AGRICULTURAL ENTERPRISES IN RURAL DEVELOPMENT STRATEGIES

TADLOCK COWAN

Novinka Books
New York

Senior Editors: Susan Boriotti and Donna Dennis
Coordinating Editor: Tatiana Shohov
Office Manager: Annette Hellinger
Graphics: Wanda Serrano and Matt Dallow
Editorial Production: Maya Colmbus, Vladimir Klestov,
                 Matthew Kozlowski and and Lorna Loperfido
Circulation: Ave Maria Gonzalez, Vera Popovic, Sean Corkery, Raymond Davis,
                 Melissa Diaz, Magdalena Nuñez, Marlene Nuñez and Jeannie Pappas
Communications and Acquisitions: Serge P. Shohov
Marketing: Cathy DeGregory

Library of Congress Cataloging-in-Publication Data

Cowan, Tadlock.
Value-added agricultural enterprises in rural development strategies / Tadlock Cowan.
     p. cm.
Includes bibliographical references and index.
     ISBN: 1-59033-819-7 (softcover)
     1. Produce trade—United States. 2. Value-added—United States. 3. Rural development—
United States. I. Title.

HD9005.C68 2003
338. 1'0973—dc22   2003020312

Copyright © 2003 by Novinka Books, An Imprint of
                 Nova Science Publishers, Inc.
                 400 Oser Ave, Suite 1600
                 Hauppauge, New York 11788-3619
                 Tele. 631-231-7269   Fax 631-231-8175
                 e-mail: Novascience@earthlink.net
                 Web Site: http://www.novapublishers.com

Printed in the United States of America

CONTENTS

PREFACE

U.S. agriculture is changing rapidly from a sector characterized by production of undifferentiated bulk commodities sold in spot markets to one of specialized markets driven by new end-user demands. As production shifts away from *commodity* agriculture to *product* agriculture, vertically integrated agribusiness firms are increasingly organizing production into *agro-food value chains* to synchronize all stages of production from used seed to supermarket. Value-added production is a central element of agro-food value chains, and control over specific "identity preserved" (IP) traits is basic to the development of product agriculture. Many farmers and ranchers are beginning to consider how they might reorganize their operations to better anticipate these changes and to participate in them, for example, by forming "new generation" value-added cooperatives, and engaging in increased contract relations with value chain integrators. Some producers see IP traits and contract production as sources of new markets, lowered risks, and higher farm and ranch incomes. Emerging opportunities for biomass-based fuels and materials processing facilities, new food processing plants, and alternative farming systems (e.g., organic) could create important new markets for producers. Smaller-scale producers too may find new opportunities in regionally-branded products, farmers markets, new specialty crops, ethnic markets, or in establishing direct marketing links between farms and regional groceries.

This book provides an overview of rural American in the 1990s and some of the socioeconomic issues facing contemporary rural areas. It discusses the role of agriculture in the rural economy and implications of the value-chains beginning to shape the contemporary structure of agriculture. It assesses the characteristics and potential of the more prominent value-added agricultural production systems as strategies for rural economic development.

Chapter 1

INTRODUCTION

Technological development and intensifying global competition are fundamentally reshaping U.S. industrial agriculture from production of undifferentiated bulk commodities sold in anonymous spot-markers to a production system of segmented and specialized markers identity-preserved (IP) commodities, value-added food products, and a focus on the end-user. This emerging shift from *commodity* agriculture to *product* agriculture, that is, from *quantity* to quality, is likely to have important effects in many rural areas, especially where large-scale, industrial agriculture remains a significant part of the economy, but, potentially, where smaller-scale production also predominates. Heightened global competition and declining profit margins in the ranchers to pursue efforts to add value to their products and, in so doing, to capture a greater part of the downstream value dominated by processing and marketing sectors. Efforts to develop and expand new types of and uses for bulk agricultural commodities (e.g., alternative fuels, bioplastics), alternative agricultural production systems (e.g., organic, intensive pasture rotation), niche markets, and specialty crops are regarded by many observes as creating new opportunities for improving the economic viability of agriculture and rural communities.[1]

---

[1] Value-added expresses the difference between the value of goods sold and the cost of materials or supplies used in producing them. The term is applied to manufacturing processes where raw commodities are initially processed into intermediate goods, which are then processed in further stages, adding increasing market value at each stage. In this report, the term retains that meaning, but also refers to other processes that add or might add market value though product differentiation. Foods grown and processed organically or in environmentally benign ways, regionally-branded food products, hormone/antibiotic-free livestock, processing waste products into goods, and renewable energy production can also constitute agricultural value-added processes and products. Value-added production in forestry and fibers is not considered in detail here, but the same logic applies to those products as well.

Expanding local processing of agricultural products has been a rural development strategy for some time. For example, soybean crushing, flour and rice milling, and beet sugar refining are long-standing value-added food manufacturing enterprises that sited their facilities near the raw material source. The value-added agriculture of today is developing in the context of vertically coordinated and integrated production systems, or *agro-food value chains,* that organize production to meet the quality assurance demands of specialized consumer markets. In such systems, IP grains (e.g., non-genetically engineered corn, high-oil corn) may be traced from grower to first-stage processor to intermediate food processor to final product on a grocery shelf or restaurant.[2] Value-added enterprises may hold significant income and risk diversification benefits for growers and ranchers across a wide spectrum of agricultural production. Traditional commodity production of high volumes at the lowest (labor) cist is characterized by low profits and the need to constantly expand the size of the farming operation. This has had significant effects in many rural areas as less competitive producers continue to leave farming. Advocates of value-added production expect value-added agriculture to create the potential for higher profit margins for producers and expanded opportunities for rural communities in processing and marketing these products to end-users, as well as stimulating grown and expansion of rural business.

Important policy issues, however, arise about the contribution these enterprises can make to reverse the economic stagnation of many rural areas, in reducing rural unemployment, in helping rural areas capture a larger share of national income, and in creating new sources of rural competitive advantage for the future. While some value-added production and marketing systems suggest new opportunities for some rural areas, other value-added production and marketing systems may produce small employment gains or do little more than shift jobs from one rural area to another. Farmer-owned manufacturing facilities that process locally produced commodities, especially commodities with high-value, IP traits, may create non-farm employment in areas where employment is scarce as well as enhance the economic viability of local businesses that service the new facilities. On the

---

[2] "Identity-preserved" (IP) products are commodities with special traits that differentiate them from other bulk commodities. IP products are traced from their site of production to final food or feed products to ensure that they are not mixed with similar undifferentiated commodities. By documenting the path from growing to final consumption of a food product, IP products can command higher prices by essentially guaranteeing their distinctiveness from non-IP products. For example, pre-packaged organic vegetables must be able to guarantee that the vegetables are grown organically and kept separated from non-organic vegetables.

other hand, other facilities (e.g., ethanol plants, soy oil, meat parking), owned by external investors, could offer relatively little in the way of long-term local development potential beyond improving incomes of some farm households selling bulk commodities to the facility or to those who find work in the manufacturing facility.

Production systems for certain value-added products may be smaller-scale operations that avoid some of the disadvantages they currently have under traditional industrial agricultural production. For example, value-added organic cooperatives may be able to achieve scale efficiencies that would elude single producers. Value-added cooperatives that can develop new alliances with consumers (e.g., farmer-grocer contracts, Internet marketing) may create new entrepreneurial opportunities for some growers and ranchers. Value-added products might also benefit from the increased attractiveness of food products grown under some form of enhanced environmental management system that can be branded or identified with a particular farm or rural area. Finally, farming and ranching operations near cities and suburban areas may be especially well-positioned to take advantage of consumer demands by serving new markets for particular agricultural products. In each of these cases, proponents believe that developing new value-added businesses in rural areas that reflect emerging changes in agriculture production may represent a successful rural economic development strategy that also preserves farming operations.

SCOPE

This report (1) providers an overview of rural America in the 1990s and some of the socioeconomic issues facing contemporary rural areas; (2) discusses the role of agriculture in the rural economy and implications of the value-chains beginning to shape the contemporary structure of agriculture; and (3) assesses the characteristics and potential of the more prominent value-added agricultural production systems as strategies for rural economic development. Three general questions serve as an organizing framework for the report:

- What are the major sources of change in rural economies today and what is the role of agriculture in local economies?

- How and where might emerging changes in value-chains and value-added agriculture affect rural development strategy in coming years?

- Could federal policies supporting value-added agricultural entrepreneurs assist rural areas in developing broader rural income growth, employment, and new sources of competitive advantage?

Value-added food-processing and industrial value-added manufacturing are the two dominant categories of agricultural value-added commodity processing. The report provides data and analysis of their potential role as a rural development strategy and concludes that their impact on employment and income is unlikely to be significant in most rural areas. Agricultural commodity processing represents a declining proportion of manufacturing activity, even as value-added manufacturing generally has tended to locate predominantly in rural areas. Large producers currently dominate such value-added enterprises as ethanol production and marketing, raising questions about the degree to which economic benefits might accrue locally.

Production of specialty crops or agricultural products produced through environmentally sound practices (e.g., organic approaches), however, may offer some small-scale producers the opportunity to develop new marketing channels, especially producers located near or within metropolitan areas. Such products are value-added in the general sense that the way they are produced can add a price premium over conventionally raised products. New markets for value-added products could create the basis for some producers to remain in farming and contribute to the overall mix of economic activities that are important to sustainable rural areas.

Significant changes in the structure of agricultural production are discussed in the report, particularly the rise of agro-food value chains. Evidence for the increasing coordination and integration of production, processing, and marketing through value-chains suggests that new organizational arrangements in farm production are developing. These developments can be seen most clearly in the increasing contract arrangement between producer and agro-food integrator. The developing importance of identity preserved (IP) products reinforces the development of agro-food value chains. The report discusses these developments and suggests that few rural areas may be able to take advantage of these structural changes, leading to further diminution of the role of agriculture in most rural economies.

CURRENT CONGRESSIONAL INTEREST

Less than 8% of the rural workforce is employed in farming and ranching today; and only 1.7% of the rural population is engaged in farming as a full-time occupation. Agriculture, however, remains the dominant vehicle through which federal rural development policies are considered.[3] Programs that enhance agricultural producer/household income are widely regarded as enhancing general rural well-being, although most observers recognize the connection has declined significantly.[4] Congress has expressed its concern with rural communities most directly through periodic omnibus farm bill legislation, most recently in the 2002 farm bill, the Farm Security and Rural Investment Act (P.L.107-171).[5] Of particular interest to Congress is the role that value-added agricultural production and other innovative enterprises might play in rural economic development strategies. Rural development titles in both House and Senate versions of the farm bill included significant provisions for development of value-added agricultural enterprises, including organic agricultural development and alternative fuels production. The House version authorized $60 million for FY2002-2011 (Sec.602) and the Senate version authorized $75 million for FY2002-2006 for value-added market development grants, with a 5% set-aside for organic products (Sec. 606). The House version also sets aside $15 million of its value-added funding for grants to establish Agriculture Innovation Centers for technical assistance to value-added agricultural businesses (Sec. 603).

In addition to these specific farm bill provisions, the 107th Congress has also shown legislative interest in other agricultural innovation and value-added agricultural production:

- H.R. 2402, the Agricultural Producers Marketing Assistance Act, would provide grants to assist value-added businesses by, among other provisions, creating an Agricultural Innovation Center demonstration project to provide technical assistance, business planning, and marketing development to start-up firms.

---

[3] The 1980 Rural Development Policy Act (P.L.96-355) designated USDA as the lead agency for coordinating rural policy; and the Department of Agriculture Reorganization Act of 1994 (P.L. 103-354) created the Office of Undersecretary of Agriculture for Rural Development to oversee rural policy.

[4] A recent survey by the W.K. Kellogg Foundation found that respondents still perceive rural America as being based on an almost completely agricultural economy. See *Perceptions of Rural America*, Kellogg Foundation. December 2001.

[5] For an overview of rural development provisions see, *A New Farm Bill: Comparing the House and Senate Proposals with Current Law*, CRS Report RL31272, February, 2002.

- Tax credits for ethanol production are included in the Investment in Value-Added Agriculture Act (S. 907), the Value-Added Development Act for American Agriculture (H.R. 1093), and the Farmers' Value-Added Agricultural Investment Tax Credit Act (H.R.1094).

- Legislation to encourage business innovation includes the Entrepreneurial Incubator Development Act of 2001 (H.R. 1418), which would provide legal, technological, and intellectual property rights assistance to small-and-medium-sized firms. The Renewable Energy from Agricultural Products (REAP) Act (H.R. 2000) would create tax credits for electricity produced from biomass and agricultural waste; and the Renewable Fuels for Energy Security Act of 2001 (S.1006) would promote fuel development from alternative sources.

- The Working Lands Stewardship Act of 2001 (H.R. 2375) would provide grants to expand the National Organic Program to include organic farming transition assistance and to establish an organic certification reimbursement program. This act would also expand State marketing programs, including set-asides for development of local and regional markets, and research for promotion of direct farmer-to-consumer marketing.

- The Agricultural Risk Protection Act of 2000 (P.L.106-224) provides research funding for developing genetically altered tobacco as a medicinal crop (Sec. 222) and for a corn-base ethanol research pilot plant (Sec. 226). The legislation also provides for $15 million in competitive grants for technical assistance and business planning for value-added agriculture product marketing.

Chapter 2

RURAL AMERICA'S NEW COMPETITIVE ENVIRONMENT

The trends and discontinuities in the character of contemporary rural America create policy issues that are fundamentally different from those of the past. When the rural sector comprised the majority of the population and agriculture was the dominant production sector, policies that improved the well-being of farmers and ranchers were *de facto* rural development policies. Farm support policies enacted during the Depression, for example, were aimed largely at reducing the significant income gap between rural and urban populations. Rural development was generally equated with reducing poverty.[1] Today, average farm household incomes are about 17% greater than the national household average; and the average net worth of farm households is double that of the national household average.[2] Rather than poverty alleviation, provision of infrastructure (e.g., highways, water, sewerage, public buildings) has come to be equated with rural development. Yet, average rural (as opposed to farm) incomes continue their historical lag behind urban incomes even as rural high-school graduation rates more closely resemble urban rates; poverty rates are higher in rural areas than they are in urban areas; and the socioeconomic economic opportunities available in many of the 2300 non-metropolitan counties in the United States has become deeply troubling to researchers, rural development practitioners, and policy makers.

---

[1] Baldwin, Sidney. *Poverty and Politics: The Rise and Decline of the Farm Security Administration*. Chapel Hill: University of North Carolina Press, 1968.

[2] Morehart, Mitch, J. Johnson, C.E. Young, G. Pompelli. "Using farm sector as a policy benchmark." *Agricultural Outlook*, June-July, 2001.

Fragmented, piecemeal programs directed at rural areas are regarded by
many researches as increasingly ineffective for creating the basis for new
competitive advantage in most rural areas. Other observers, especially in
heavily rural and farming-dependent states, believe that a renewed emphasis
on agriculture can become an effective rural development strategy. Sectoral
emphasis, whether agriculture or manufacturing, have not produced the
kinds of growth and generalized social welfare that rural advocates had
hoped for ever the past 30 years. The search for comprehensive, integrated
rural development policies and strategies that might alter this picture
represents an increasingly complex political economic challenge for policy
makers and rural citizens.

DEMOGRAPHIC OVERVIEW OF
NON-METROPOLITAN AMERICA

Any discussion of rural areas or rural policy must begin with the caveat
that the great diversity characterizing rural places presents an immediate
barrier to any facile generalization about Rural America. USDA's county
typology of the 2,300 non-metro counties in Tables 1 and 2, although the
data are somewhat dated, provides one useful approach to understanding
rural diversity for descriptive and policy purposes.

Table 1. USDA Classification of Non-metro Counties by Economic Type

Economic Type	Definition	Number of Counties (1989 data)
Farming-dependent	20% or more of total labor and proprietors' income from agriculture	556 (These counties had decreased to 312 in 1999, or approximately 13% of all non-metro counties).
Manufacturing-dependent	Greater than or equal to 30% of total income from manufacturing	506
Mining-dependent	Greater than or equal to 20% of total income from mining	146
Government-dependent	Greater than or equal to 25% of total income from government	244
Service-dependent	50% or more of total income from service sector employment	323
Non-specialized	Not classified as an economically specialized county	484

Source: Cook, Peggy J. and Karen L. Mizer. *The Revised ERS County Typology*. USDA-ERS,
     November. 1994.
Note: Economic and policy types can and do overlap

Table 2. USDA Classification of Non-metro Countries by Policy Type

Policy Type	Definition	Number of Counties (1989 data)
Transfer-dependent	25% or more of personal income from Federal/State/Local transfer Payments (weighted average)	381
Retirement-destination	Population aged 60 and older increased 15% or more during 1980-1990	190
Persistent Poverty	20% or more of county population in each of 4 Census years: 1960, 1970, 1980, 1990 with poverty-level income	535
Commuting	40% or more of county's workers commuting outside their county of residence in 1990	381
Federal lands	30% of county's land area federally owned in 1987	270

Source: Cook, Peggy J. and Karen L. Mizer. *The Revised ERS County Typology*. USDA-ERS, November. 1994.

Note: Economic and policy types can and do overlap

BOX 1: WHAT IS RURAL?

Rural and non-metropolitan populations have often been treated as synonyms. Metro and non-metro areas are defined by USDA on the basis of counties. Metro areas contain (1) core counties with one or more central cities of at least 50,000 or with a Census Bureau defined urbanized area (and a total metro population of 100,000 or more) and (2) fringe counties that are economically tied to the core counties. Non-metro counties are defined as those places either outside the boundaries of metro areas or towns with populations under 50,000. Rural areas comprise places with open territory and fewer than 2,500 residents. Urban areas comprise larger places and densely settled areas around them. As the relation between metro and non-metro areas becomes more complex, researches are beginning to use more precise categories, e.g., non-metro adjacent/non-metro non-adjacent areas, rural urban commuting codes, etc.

See John B. Cromartie and Linda L. Swanson, "Census tracts more precisely define rural population and areas." *Rural Development Perspectives*, Vol. 11, 3, pp.31-39, May, 2001.

Urban expansion and the globalization of markets are key sources of contemporary rural change. Proximity to urban areas transforms rural areas, physically in terms of land use and settlement patterns, and socially in terms of labor markets, transportation systems, and demography. Indeed, the rural-urban dichotomy is arguably even less helpful analytically today in urban-adjacent areas because there is such extensive flow of goods, people, and ideas between rural and urban places.[3] Yet, conventional rural development thinking and planning have made a sharp distinction between rural and urban often without attending to other important spatial and political dimensions, for example, regional interactions. The rural proportion of the population still tends to be regarded largely as a residual category, i.e., those areas that are not within a Metropolitan Statistical Area (MSA) as defined by the Bureau of the Census and/or the Office of Management and Budget, *or* are cities and towns with populations greater than 50,000 (Box 1). Even USDA's Office of Rural Development uses different definitions of "rural" to administer its programs. Business development loans, for example, can go to communities with as many as 50,000 people; wastewater grants and loans may go to towns smaller than 10,000; and loans to build hospitals and fire stations may be targeted to communities of 20,000 or less. Special technical assistance grants can be reserved for rural areas as small as 2,500.

While the U.S., as other advanced industrial economies, may be considered "post-rural" across a broad spectrum of cultural and socioeconomic criteria, approximately 55 million persons lived in non-metropolitan/rural areas in 2001. This is nearly 20% of the U.S. population. This proportion has remained surprisingly contract over the past century. After years of little or no population growth, rural and small towns grew faster than suburban and urban areas in the 1970s. In the 1980s, however, this trend reversed during the general recession and farm crisis, and the number of retirees moving to rural areas declined. Non-metro population grew by just 1.3 million, or 2.7% during the 1980s. A shift occurred again during the 1990s with the non-metro population growing by 3.9 million, or 7.6% from April, 1990 to July, 1999, although growth was not as pronounced as it was in the 1970s. All non-metro net growth in the 1990s is the product of migration; the annual rate of natural (i.e., birth and death) as opposed to immigration growth fell by a third in non-metro counties during the 1990s.[4]

Non-metro population growth was highest in the Mountain West and lowest or non-existent in the Great Plains, Mississippi Delta, and Corn Belt. Much of this growth stemmed from metro residents relocating to adjoining

---

[3] Tacoli, Cecilia. "Rural-urban interactions: A guide to the literature." *Environment and Urbanization* 10(1): 147-166, 1998.

[4] Calvin Beale. "Nonmetro population growth rate recedes in a time of unprecedented national prosperity." *Rural Conditions and Trends*, 11(2). December, 2000.

non-metro areas and from other sources of immigration. A significant portion of contemporary rural migration also stems Hispanic immigrants arriving to take jobs in agriculture-related industries such as meat product manufacturing. Non-metro counties adjoining metro areas accounted for almost two-thirds of all non-metro growth, increasing about 12% on average over the decade. Despite this net inflow of people from metro areas, the rate net migration into rural areas, which had steadily increased during the early and mid-1990s, dropped to about 0.5% from 1997-1999. The number of non-metro counties with decreasing population rose from 600 from 1990-1995 to 855 in 1999.[5] This more recent decrease in rural migration also occurred among college graduates, although the number of college graduates entering rural areas was slightly higher than those graduates leaving (Table 3). Although overall non-metro population change is not fully determined by migration for economic reasons, many low-growth farming dependent areas that lack the attraction of natural amenities such as those found in the Mountain West of Florida, are unlikely to experience future population growth without new sources of non-farm employment. Growth in many metropolitan areas, however, will also bring many rural areas into urban labor markets with potentially important social and economic changes for rural areas.

Table 3. Average Annual Adult Non-Metropolitan Net Migration Rates By Educational Level, 1977-1999

	Less than High School Degree	High School Degree	College Graduate	All Adults (25 years and older)
In	2.38%	3.30%	4.40%	3.31%
Out	1.67%	2.50%	4.20%	2.20%
Net	0.71%	0.73%	0.20%	0.62%

Source: USDA-ERS calculations from Bureau of Labor Statistics, 1998 Current Population Surveys.

INCOME AND EMPLOYMENT
TRENDS IN RURAL AREAS

Rural earnings growth reflects a continuing national trend of rising real earnings in both metro and non-metro labor markets. The rise in women's

---

[5] Ibid., p.29.

earnings is the primary component of the rural labor market increases from
1990-1997. Real weekly average earnings in 1997 dollars for women rose
8.5%, while men's real weekly earnings rose by less than 1%.[6] Despite the
strength of the economic expansion during the 1990s, however, over 25%of
rural wage and salary workers earned full-time-equivalent wages below the
poverty level for a family of four in 1999 ($17,000). Since the early 1990s,
rural earnings growth generally has outpaced urban earnings growth, due, in
part, to the sluggish recovery from the early 1990s recession in urban areas.
Earnings among the lowest paid rural workers, however, have risen more
slowly than for the rest of the labor force even as their education levels have
increased.

In 1997, rural areas lagged behind urban areas by at least $9,000 in real
per capita income. This gap has widened since the late 1980s, exacerbated by
the loss of manufacturing jobs, which tend to pay higher wages than
agriculture or rural consumer service and recreation jobs. The rural-urban
earnings gap was more than 30% grater in 1995 than it was in 1977.[7]
Earnings per job also remain consistently and substantially lower in rural
areas than in urban and the gap has steadily increased over the past decade
(Table 4).

In part, lower rural earnings may reflect the lower college graduation
rates of rural workers, although, as noted earlier, high-school completion
rates have come close to matching those of urban areas. Another possible
explanation is that income returns to education are generally lower in rural
than in urban areas.[8] The proportion of low-wage employment in rural areas
actually increased over the past decade. Local officials and business elites
eager to promote a "pro-business" environment can also be very influential
in determining the types of employers that locate to rural areas. The
manufacturing operations that have relocated to many rural areas, e.g.,
branch plant assembly, textiles, metal fabrication, for example, are
predominantly non-union and generally require lower-skilled workers than
urban manufacturing jobs. The fact that rural areas have also seen growth in
economically vulnerable populations, e.g., minorities and single female-
headed households, may also partly explain the metro/non-metro gap in real

[6] USDA's Economic Research Service calculations from the Current Population Survey data,
1997.
[7] Rhodes, Douglas and Mitch Renkow. "Explaining rural-urban earnings differentials in the
U.S." Paper presented at Annual Meetings of the American Agricultural Economics
Association, Salt Lake City, Utah. 1998
[8] Renkow, Mitch. "Income non-convergence and rural-urban income differentials: Evidence
from North Carolina" Southern Economic Journal 62, 1996.

earnings per job, although by a substantial margin, most rural poor are not minorities.

Table 4. Earnings Per Non-Farm Job, 1989-1999

YEAR	METRO	NON-METRO	NON-METRO AS PERCENT OF METRO
1989	$32,206	$23,819	74.0%
1990	$32,239	$23,561	73.1%
1991	$32,264	$23,489	72.8%
1992	$33,449	$24,045	71.9%
1993	$33,346	$24,032	72.1%
1994	$33,458	$24,094	72.0%
1995	$33,469	$23,788	71.1%
1996	$33,798	$23,763	70.3%
1997	$34,502	$24,150	70.0%
1998	$35,745	$24,843	69.5%
1999	$36,684	$25,201	68.7%

Source: USDA-ERS calculations from Bureau of Economic Analysis data.
Note: In constant 1999 dollars

Current low-wage employment rates in rural areas remain higher than in the late 1970s despite a better educated workforce and a very low national unemployment rate. This may suggest that public policies that attend primarily to improving the employability of workers in at least some rural areas may not be effective in and of themselves. Although most low-wage workers are women, men's share of low-wage work in rural areas has risen over the past 20 years. Despite an increase in job growth in late 1998, the pace of employment growth in rural areas slowed from an average of 1.8% between 1990 and 1995 to about 1.5% in 1999.

RURAL POVERTY

The poverty rate for rural areas in 1999 was higher than that for urban areas (14.3% versus 11.2%). The changing location of economic activities within the U.S. and across international border, technological changes, and stagnant or falling real minimum wage rates have been especially hard on those rural areas where large clusters of low-wage workers reside. Over 500 rural counties (23%) are defines by the 1997 Census of Agriculture as being in "persistent poverty." These counties had 20% or more of their populations at or below persistently poor counties are in the Southeast and Delta regions, Native American reservations, core Appalachia, and the lower Rio Grande Valley. Agriculture is often a significant economic sector in those regions, but as with national trends, its role has declined. A large pool of poorly educated residents, high proportions of minorities, and the presence of mostly low-wage manufacturing and part-time service employment in persistently poor counties help explain why these areas have found it very difficult to improve the livelihoods of residents.

Few attractive employment options, poorly educated workers, substandard housing, and inadequate public infrastructure characterize persistent poverty counties where, in addition, the majority of limited-resource and minority farmers also reside. Many poor rural areas have low-wage employment opportunities at best, long distances to services and jobs and lower automobile access, little public transportation, and lack of childcare options.[9] Persistently low per capita incomes often translate into low levels of human capital investment. With little growth in rural high-skill employment opportunities and downward pressure on wages in low-skilled employment, many persistent-poverty counties, especially in the South, appear to be very badly positioned to reverse these trends.[10] Some observers have also concluded that rural poverty in certain states, e.g., California, is actually being re-created through immigration, driven, in part, by the expansion of low-wage, immigrant intensive agriculture.[11]

Rural Diversity is Significant

Rural experience may be highly variable from county to county and from region to region. Highly aggregated socioeconomic indicators can often be misleading. Average job growth, unemployment rates, earnings in many rural areas adjacent to metro areas are often as high as those within metro areas. But this may be due in part to the fact that many of the jobs in adjacent

[9] Informal work, i.e., unrecorded labor, is often an important source of income in rural areas. Welfare reform legislation's work mandates do not recognize work in the informal sector. Thus, rural residents in very poor areas are doubly burdened by the loss of welfare support without necessarily being able to replace their lost income through employment in the formal sector.
[10] Nord, Mark. "*Overcoming persistent poverty – and sinking into it: income trends in persistent poverty and other high poverty rural counties, 1989-1994.*" *Rural Development Perspectives*, 12 (3), 1997:2-10.
[11] Taylor, J. Edward, Phillip Martin, and Michael Fix. *Poverty Amid Prosperity: Immigration and the Changing Face of Rural California.* Urban Institute, Washington, DC, 1997.

non-metro areas within commuting distance to urban areas are service related, especially business services, or high-skilled manufacturing employment, jobs which pay higher wages on average. Other rural areas, e.g., Native American reservations, may have unemployment rates of up to 75% although *average* metro and non-metro unemployment rates are similar (4.3% vs. 4.6% respectively in 2001).[12] Rural communities that captured some of the spillover of urban affluence did well in the 1990s, and may be able to maintain that advantage if they increase their proportion of high-wage service sector employment. For many other rural communities, however, especially those remote from urban areas, lacking amenities, or with a high proportion of poorly educated working-age residents, the 1990s offered little change. Moreover, future prospects remain bleak in many of these areas unless there are significant changes in local and regional institutions, infrastructure, and entrepreneurial capacity.[13]

---

[12] Rates are based on civilian, non-institutional populations, 16 years and older, 2nd Quarter, 2001. Bureau of Labor Statistics.

[13] Duncan, Cynthia. *Worlds Apart: Why Poverty Persist in Rural America.* New Haven: Yale University Press, 1999.

Chapter 3

AGRO-FOOD VALUE CHAINS AND VALUE-ADDED AGRICULTURAL ENTERPRISES

VALUE-ADDED MANUFACTURING IN RURAL AREAS

Preserving family farms and increasing rural household incomes through the creation of new value-added agricultural opportunities has been a goal of policy makers throughout much of the 20th century. Yet, the agriculture sector has continued to decline in importance in rural economies along with the decline in the number of farm household. The structure of labor in non-metro areas reveals agriculture's declining role. Manufacturing and consumer and producer services account for over half the share of rural earnings today (Table 5). Average non-farm agriculturally-related employment also lags well behind average earnings for the private sector as a whole in non-metro areas (Table 6).

Table 5. Share of Rural Earnings by Employment Sector, 1999

Employment Sector	Percentage of Rural Earnings
Consumer Services	23%
Manufacturing	21%
Public Sector	20%
Producers Services	9%
Agriculture, Forestry, Fishing	5%
Recreation	4%

Source: ERS calculations from Bureau of Labor Statistics, 1999

Table 6. Average Non-farm Wage and Salary Earning per Job by Industry Group, 1997

Industry Sector	Non-metro	Metro
Agriculture Services, forestry, fishing	16,633	16,219
Mining	$39419	$44,510
Construction	$20,969	$28,076
Manufacturing	$27,832	$35,318
Value-added	$25,345	$28,989
Routine	$26,912	$31,324
technology		
High-tech	$31,580	$40,524
Producer services	$24,389	$38,334
Communications	$35,463	$49,076
Business/professional services	$19,380	$30,092
Finance and insurance	$28,486	$53,379
Transportation, utilities, and wholesale trade	$27,167	$35,101
Recreation	$8,741	$11,263
Consumer services	$16,157	$21,459
Total private sector	$21,264	$29,105

Source: ERS calculations based on County Business Patterns enhanced data file.

If value-added agricultural production is to modify these trends in the future, economic development specialists and policy makers will need to examine closely the commercial potential of new products, the dynamics plant location, and a range of possible impacts from pursuing a value-added development strategy based on agriculture.

Value-added manufacturing industries in all production sectors are vitally important to rural areas. New capital investments in value-added industries, while modest during the 1990s, were relatively more concentrated in rural than in urban areas.[1] While the national economy has become more service-oriented in the past 25 years, and imports now account for an increasing share of manufactured goods, manufacturing's share of the rural economy has remained relatively strong. Since the early 1950s, manufacturing was regarded by economic development practitioners and policy makers as the key source of jobs to replace those being lost in agriculture. Import competition in the 1980s led many metropolitan

[1] Canning, Patrick. "Investment patterns indicate modest expansion by value-added industries." Rural Conditions and Trends, Vol. 8., No.3 March, 198.

manufacturing firms to move some of their operations to rural areas to take advantage of lower labor costs, property taxes, and land costs. This had the advantage of replacing jobs in textile and leather goods plants that many rural areas lost to foreign locations. Today, manufacturing is relatively more important to rural areas than to metro areas; and more rural counties today depend on manufacturing than on agriculture-related employment or services. Nearly 75% of manufacturing plants in the U.S. employ 500 or fewer workers, with many of the high-wage rural manufacturing plants being branches of larger organizations.

Manufacturing provides approximately 17% of all rural jobs, with nearly a third of that rural manufacturing wage and salary workforce worked in value-added industries in 1996.[2] The proportion of value-added employment has remained fairly steady during the 1990s. Value-added manufacturing generally, including that related to agriculture, grew faster in non-metro areas than in metro areas, although rural value-added industries rely more on the less educated, pay lower wages, and have higher proportions of immigrant workers than do other manufacturing industries.[3] Lower education levels in value-added labor in metro regions as well suggest that value-added industry in general is dominated by less-educated workers relative to other manufacturing. Low real earnings growth in rural value-added industries reflected the earnings of the rural work force as a whole during the 1990s. While non-metro value-added workers earn less than other manufacturing workers, their wages are significantly higher than non-metro consumer service jobs, in part, because the latter are more likely to be part-time.[4] Food processing industries account for 43% of value-added jobs and pay the lowest wages ($24,000) of value-added manufacturing. Rural areas maintained or increased their share of jobs in almost all farm-related value-added manufacturing sectors.

Value-added employment in general grew faster in rural areas than it did nationally during the period 1989-1994; and farm-related value-added accounted for much of this gain.[5] With the exception of meat product and grain product manufacturing, farm-related value-added manufacturing employment fell nationally between 1989-1994. During this period,

---

[2] Gibbs, Robert, "Value-added workers earn less, have less education than other rural manufacturing workers." *Rural Conditions and Trends*, Vol. 8, No. 3, March, 1998.
[3] *Ibid.*
[4] Unlike consumer services, producer services are a relatively small part of the rural economy and they pay much less in rural than urban areas. This is particularly true of the finance and insurance industries, where non-metro pay is only 53% of metro pay.
[5] Value-added agricultural manufacturing is defined as 20% or more of farm products used in intermediaries.

however, farm-related value-added employment increased 8.5% in non-metro areas. Other manufacturing employment in non-metro areas increased only 1.2%. While the number of farm-related value-added establishments increased by over 4% from 1989-1994, other non-metro manufacturing establishments increased by 13.3%.[6] The influx of Hispanic workers into some rural areas in the 1990s can, in part, be explained by the expansion of the value-added meat production sector.

The meat production manufacturing sector led employment growth among farm value-added industries; Hispanic employees were a significant source of these workers as the meat packing industry had left the urban Midwest and Northeast for lower cost nonunion labor in the rural South and Great Plains.[7] Meat packing plants also seem to have an impact on local economies beyond the packing facility itself through the strength of their background linkages in the local and regional economy. Plants in value-added industries generally are more likely than other manufacturing enterprises to purchase materials locally because they are material-intensive operations. Although estimating income multipliers is a very inexact exercise where final estimates can very enormously depending on model assumptions, food-processing plants appear to have among the highest spending locally per job, even though earnings in food processing jobs are the lowest of all manufacturing subsectors. Table 7, based on data from a USDA survey, indicates that an important local economic stimulus derives from value-added food manufacturing.

AGRICULTURE IN THE RURAL ECONOMY

As an important source of rural jobs and income, agriculture's role has declined significantly over the past 60 years. In rural areas today, less than 8% of the workforce is employed in farming and agricultural services (e.g., landscaping, horticultural services, veterinary services, soil preparation and crop services). Most household income for most farm families now comes from off-farm sources; only about 13% of farm households receive more than 80% of their household income from farming.[8] While the extent of dependency as measured by jobs in the food and fiber system varies

---

[6] Gale, Fred. "Most value-added manufacturing increased its attachment to rural areas during 1989-1994." *Rural Conditions and Trends.* Vo. 8, No. 3, March, 1998.
[7] *Ibid.*
[8] Mishra, Ashok and Mitchell Morehart. "Farm families' savings: Findings from the ARMS Survey." *Agricultural Outlook,* April, 2002.

significantly by region, only 1.7% of rural residents identify farming as their primary occupation. Net farm income today amounts to only 2-3% of total non-metro personal income. In only one state, South Dakota, does agriculture account for at least 10% of gross state production, while ranking only 45th among states in food and fiber employment.

Table 7. Estimated Local Expenditure by Nonmetro Agricultural Value-Added Manufacturing Plants, 1995

Industry	Local purchases (millions $)	Salaries and Wages (millions $)	Jobs (number)	Local spending per job ($)
Meat packing	$32.5	$7.6	370	$108,500
Poultry processing	$15.4	$7.0	467	$48,100
Dairy products	$12.7	$1.9	91	$160,000
Preserved fruits and vegetables	$12.8	$3.8	229	$72,500
Grain mill products	$4.4	$1.2	53	$105,200
Bakery products	$0.6	$4.6	208	$24,900
Sugar and confectionary	$10.1	$4.3	236	$60,900
Fats and oils	$25.7	$2.1	86	$323,600
Beverages	$3.4	$2.1	88	$62,700

Source: Estimates by USDA-ERS; 1995 data, not adjusted for inflation. Local purchases, wages, and numbers of jobs are from the 1996 Rural Manufacturing Survey; material expenditures and non-production worker salaries are from 1995 Annual Survey of Manufactures.

As is the case within metro areas, the service sector is the largest source of jobs in rural areas today. Farming-dependent counties (those where 20% or more of labor and proprietors' income is derived from farming) dwindled to approximately 300 counties by the mid-1990s, mostly in the Western Corn Belt, Great Plains, and parts of the Southeast and Northwest, down from 556 counties in 1989. During the 1990s, farm-dependent counties also saw continued population losses and economic growth rates below the average for all rural counties.

As a share of the national economy, farming, and agriculture more broadly, counties its long-term path of decline. Farm employment fell for non-metro areas in all U.S. regions, declining on average by nearly 27% from 1975 to 1996 (Table 8). Moreover, in some rural areas (e.g., North Dakota, South Dakota, Iowa), farm employment losses were grater than job gains in farm-related employment.

Table 8. Decline in Farm Employment, 1975-1996

Region	Number of Farming Jobs Lost, 1975-1996 (1)	Percent Change, 1975-1996
Total U.S. Non-Metro	**666,783**	**-26.9**
Appalachia	115.117	-30.9
Corn Belt	169,926	-32.1
Delta States	75,475	-38.3
Lake States	73,094	-28.0
Mountain	18,540	-12.6
Northeast	28,567	-26.1
Northern Plains	68,904	-25.3
Pacific	3,861	-3.6
Southeast	87,868	-43.2
Southern Plains	23,187	-8.7

Source: USDA-ERS calculations based on Department of Commerce data
(1) Includes farm proprietor, wage and salaried farm workers

The Bureau of Labor Statistics projects a 0.1% decline per year in agriculture employment between 1998 and 2008, which includes a 13% decline in employment of farmers, the largest projected decline of any occupation.[9] Employment of farm workers is projected to decline 6.6%. Employment growth in food and kindred products manufacturing is projected to rise only about 2% between 1998 and 2008 with most growth in meat products.[10] Non-farm employment, on the other hand, is projected to grow 14% between 1998 and 2008, mostly in the service sector. Employment in the agricultural output sector, e.g., processing, marketing, and distribution, is expected to grow somewhat, but at a slower rate than that of most other industries.

Over the past 30 years, geographic concentration of fewer and larger farms, declining employment opportunities, and associated population decline have left many small communities across the county simply non-viable. In many rural areas, the loss of farm jobs has not been accompanied by creation of enough new non-farm jobs to retain rural populations. Although jobs in farming have declined steadily for some time, jobs in food retail ad wholesale sectors have grown. Agricultural wholesale and retail trade have provided most of the new farm-related jobs in non-metro areas

---

[9]Allison Thomson. " Industry Output and Employment Projections to 2008." *Monthly Labor Review*, November, 1999.
[10] *Ibid.*

over the past two decades. Continued growth in these sectors, however, depends on population growth and an expanding consumer market. Food retail and wholesale activities lend to locate close to consumer markets, so much of the observed national growth in agriculture-related employment may have occurred in non-metro areas near urbanized areas. Farm-dependent counties, located largest in states with populations too sparse to support strong retail growth, have gained relatively few of these jobs (Table 9).

**Table 9. U.S. Non-Metro Agricultural-Related
Employment Change, 1975-1996**

INDUSTRIAL SECTOR	NUMBER OF JOBS	PERCENT CHANGE, 1975-1996
Farming	-666,783	-26.9
Forestry, fisheries, and agricultural services (1)	100,868	114.0
Agricultural Inputs	-28,083	-11.7
Processing and Marketing	-100,179	-8.63
Wholesale and Retail Trade	1,310,566	94.7
Indirect Agribusiness (2)	35,977	34.5

Source: USDA-ERS
(1) Most agricultural service increases were in veterinarian and crop services
(2) Chemical and fertilizer mining, food products machinery, miscellaneous textile products, paper and pulpwood products

AGRICULTURAL COMMODITY PROCESSING:
THE CASE OF IOWA

Research on the structure of traditional value-added agricultural industries is useful in assessing the contribution this sector play in states and regions where agriculture is prominent in the economy. It may also suggest the role value-added production might play in rural areas in the future inasmuch as these industries will provide a base on which to expand value-added production or to develop new kinds of production. To take one illustrative example, value-added agriculture already has a strong presence in Iowa, a major farm state. Increasing vale-added production has, more recently, become a central objective within Iowa's economic development strategy.[11] Iowa agricultural producers and officials have expressed the

---

[11] This section draws heavily from an input-output analysis of agricultural processing industries in Iowa. While limitations of single case studies should be borne in mind, case studies do

understandable hopes that value-added agricultural production will provide high-wage jobs and more off-farm employment, create new sources of farm income for small farming operations, and make the state more attractive to job seekers.

Agricultural commodity processing (ACP) industries manufacture raw commodities into value-added food and industrial products, some of which are intermediate processed commodities that become the inputs to other human and animal food products. While a complete list of ACP industries would also include leather and leather products and chemicals and chemical products, 95% of Iowa's employment in ACP industries is in 35 food and kindred products industries, e.g., meat and dairy processing, grain and soybean processing, frozen foods, bakery products, animal feeds, and soft drinks. Meat processing (e.g., packing plants, sausage and prepared meat production, slaughtering and processing) represented more than 50% of all Iowa processing jobs in 1998. Grain processing e.g., flour and other grain milling, cereal breakfast food, wet corn milling, and prepared animal feed, represented just over 20% of all food processing jobs in 1998.

Between 1992 and 1998, food and kindred products industries together accounted for about 20% of all manufacturing jobs in the state, but less than 4% of all non-farm jobs in the state. Two other measures for comparing ACP economic outcomes to the rest of the Iowa economy are (1) industrial output and (2) value-added. Figure 1 compares these two measures in the ACP industries to those in agriculture and agricultural service industries, and other manufacturing sectors. The ACP provided the least employment and value-added production of all manufacturing industries in the state in 1997. Industrial output from ACP and agriculture generally was between one-half and one-third that of employment, output, and value-added for all other manufacturing industries. Not only did ACP industries contribute less to Iowa's economy relative to other manufacturing industries, they are growing more slowly than other manufacturing sectors. ACP industries grew at a rate only slightly more than a third of the manufacturing sector's average growth rate between 1992 to 1998. Employment grew by 14.5% in the manufacturing sector as a whole; it grew only 5.5% in the ACP industries. While 4,900 new ACP jobs were added to Iowa's economy from 1992-1998, these gains were offset by the loss of 2,100 jobs contracting ACP industries,

serve to highlight broad characteristics that may be salient in other areas as well. See Eathington, Liesl, D. Swenson, D. Otto. "Employment growth in Iowa's agricultural commodity processing industries, 1992-1998." Department of Economics, Iowa State University, 2000.
Web location: www.econ.iastate.edu/research/webpapers/ND0081.doc.

leaving a net growth in ACP employment in Iowa of 2,800 new jobs. Meat processing industries added 350 new jobs between 1992 and 1998; but there was a net loss of 800 jobs in gain and soybean processing, mostly occurring in the feed industry.

The national trends noted in Table 7 above are equally evident in Iowa. Between 1992 and 1998, employment in Iowa's ACP industries fell from 22% to 20% of total manufacturing employment. Not only did total employment in ACP industries fall, the distribution and concentration of ACP employment also varied.

**Figure 1: ACP and Other Industry
Contribution to Iowa's Economy, 1997**

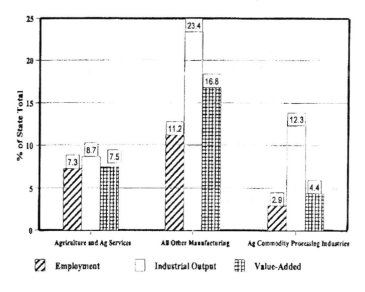

Most ACP jobs were located in Iowa's 10 metro counties, with 11,100 jobs in the 11 urban counties and 17,500 in the state's 60 smaller urban counties. Iowa's rural counties, e.g., those outside metro areas or in towns with less than 50,000 in habitants, had just under 2,400 ACP jobs in 1998.

One of value-added agriculture's hoped-for results is improved non-farm rural employment. But most Iowa ACP industries are slow-growing or declining. Slow employment growth rates as well as plant location preferences in ACP industries suggest that these industries may be limited in the amount of future employment and economic growth they can reasonably be expected to generate within Iowa's rural areas. The authors of a recent

Iowa study of agricultural processing concluded that "... agricultural commodity processing industries have an undeniably important role in (Iowa's) economic activity. However, expectations about their promise for Iowa's economic future have been growing far more rapidly than the industries themselves."[12]

AGRO-FOOD VALUE CHAINS

Long-standing trends toward fewer, larger, and more specialized commercial farms and ranchers in the U.S. (horizontal integration) are well documented. Not only have these trends been observed for many years, recent data suggest they may be accelerating as pressures increase from global competitors and as new agricultural technologies continue to reinforce the substitution of capital for labor. Some researchers have argued that current trends are leading to a farm structure where 10,000-acre corn farms may soon become the economically efficient size unit for that commodity.[13] Rapid and increasing consolidation and coordination and deepening vertical integration in agriculture are indicators of a more fundamental restructuring occurring in the global food and fiber system today. A growing share of commodity producers, mostly within animal production currently, are joining supply chains.[14] A supply chain is a tightly organized production system formed by agribusiness firms that, in its most coordinated form, could potentially link each step of food production from proprietary genetic material to the grocery shelf. Broiler production is the exemplar of this trend. Approximately 40 firms now contract to produce 97% of all broilers. These trends are appearing increasingly in pork production and are beginning in cash grains.

A distinguishing characteristic of supply chains is their reliance on contractual agreements, licenses, joint ventures, integrated ownership, and other business arrangements with different segments of the agro-food system. These alliances with producers may permit contracting firms to by-pass more traditional commodity markets. To better insulate themselves from price volatility and dwindling markets, many commodity producers are abandoning their independent operations and adopting contract commodity

---

[12] Ibid., p. 29.
[13] National Corn Growers Association. *Changes in the Evolution of Corn Belt Agriculture.* February, 2002.
[14] Drabenstott, Mark. "Rural America in a new century." *Main Street Economist,* Federal Reserve Bank of Kansas City, October, 1999.

production and marketing arrangements with agribusiness firms. According to the USDA's Economic Research Service, about 35% of the total value U.S. agricultural production in 1998 was produced under some form of contractual arrangement.[15] Over half of large family farms are involved in some form of contracting and these farms accounted for over 66% of the total value of commodities under contract.[16] Over 90% of the total value of contract production was in 10 commodity groups: soybeans, corn, fruit, vegetable, nursery, cotton, cattle, hogs, poultry, and dairy.

The growth of supply chains has implications for many rural areas because of their potential for creating geographically specific production sectors in agriculture that some observes, have characterized as a hub, spoke, and wedge cluster.[17] For example, a livestock-processing plant located at a hub is built near livestock-feeling operations. These feeding operations are supplied by mills drawing their grain and oilseed through transportation and communication spokes connecting crop production "wedges" in the periphery. Few clusters may be needed to supply the demand. Many farming areas that might wish to become a "hub" may not be able to assemble the necessary capital and managerial services to do so. While the Great Plains has certain social and environmental characteristics that might make the region compatible with large-scale animal operations (e.g., sparse populations), it is likely that only a few hubs will be economically feasible under supply chain arrangements. Other counties, e.g., Canada, may also become increasingly competitive as supply hubs. Some industry observes believe that under a supply chain arrangement, for example, 50 or fewer pork producers and 12 state-of-the-art packing plants could, in the near future, supply the entire U.S. pork market.[18] Peripheral farms will continue their trend toward larger and fewer units and will require less and less labor and other local inputs. Integrated ownership of a supply hub could displace resources from traditional farms and rural areas.[19]

[15] USDA. *Agricultural Resource Management Study,* 1998
[16] Ibid.
[17] Drabenstott, Mark and L.G. Meeker. "Consolidation in U.S. agriculture: the new rural landscape and public policy." *Economic Review,* Kansas City Federal Reserve, October, 1999.
[18] Benjamin, G. *"Industrialization in hog production: implications for Midwest agriculture."* Economic Perspectives, Federal Reserve Bank of Chicago, 1997.
[19] Opposition to these industrialization trends is also widespread because concentration and consolidation in the agro-food industry continues to be regarded as significant threat to the survival of small, family farms. See Heffernan, William. *Consolidation in the Food and Agriculture System.* Report to the National Farmers Union. February, 1999.

Commodity supply chains are evolving into integrated *agro-food value chains*. Value chains are linked networks of agribusiness firms and actors managing each phase from production to consumption. Value chains, in contract to supply chains, are consumer driven and more closely integrate production, processing, marketing, and distribution (Table 10). With increased proprietary control over new technologies, agribusiness firms are developing the means to exercise grater control over each phase of the food production process by synchronizing every stage from tillage to table. Of central importance to a value chain is the capacity to assure quality and traceability throughout the chain by identity-presented (IP) production for specific end-users.

Table 10. Comparison of Agricultural Supply and Value Chains

SUPPLY CHAINS	VALUE CHAINS
Producer oriented	Consumer oriented
Supply driven	Demand driven
Focus on quantity	Focus on quality
Focus on cost	Focus on value
Anonymous sourcing	Identity presented
Bulk volume management	Small volume management
Many independent decisions	Few cascading decisions
Open to many producers	Closed to most producers

IDENTITY PRESENTED AGRICULTURAL PRODUCTS

As a coordinated production system, agro-food value chains manage the sequence of value-adding activities from raw commodity to end use. During the shift to mass production and distribution in the late 19th century, processing and packaging became the means by which manufacturers branded their products to differentiate them from other similar mass produced items. The current evolution of value chains is moving the importance of identifying and tracing the ingredients that go into food products to the upstream raw commodity producer. Identity preservation (IP) of agricultural products, e.g., non-genetically engineered or organic commodities, can confer value premiums by assuring the end user that such grains are traced though each stage of food production (Box 2). Nominally undifferentiated corn and soybeans have, for example, enough naturally occurring variability to potentially justify 10-30 cents-per bushel value differentials.[20] This premium, however, is less than the expected costs of special trait preservation, which is likely to mean that most of these grains will still be handled as bulk grains in the system. Research has suggested that grains of high-value (more than 50 cents per bushel) justify the costs of non-traditional IP tracing and handing methods such as segregation though testing and monitoring shipments throughout the value chain.[21]

BOX 2. IDENTITY PRESERVATION FOOD PRODUCTS

The restaurant TGI Friday features Meyer Natural Angus beef at its restaurants. These cattle are raised without hormones or antibiotics and are not fed with feed containing animal by products. A single-source of origin permits monitoring from field to restaurants.

Value-enhanced grains (VEG) include white corn, food-grade yellow corn, and waxy corn. Frito Lay contracts with producers for white corn to make its Fritos Corn Chips. The company tracks the processed corn through all stages on a big by bag basis.

See: Martinez, Steve and David E. Davis, Farm Business Practices. Coordinate Production with Consumer Preferences. *FoodReview*, 25, 1, Spring, 2002.

Trade Issues

Because many consumers today have greater choice over where their food comes from and how it is produced, value chains agribusiness the organizational structure both for creating new markets and for meeting the demands of these consumers. Specially-driven product markets will require sophisticated means of traceability and special handing. For example, genetically engineered product tracing and labeling are becoming an increasingly important factor in exporting not only raw commodities, but also animal feeds and food products. Taiwan, Australia/New Zealand, Japan, South Korea, and China each have or will have within the year, mandatory genetically engineered product labeling laws specifying minimum tolerances. Under such regulatory regimes, documenting the source of a

---

[20] Hurburgh, Charles R. Jr. *Initiation of end-user specific grain marketing in Iowa elevators.* MATRIC Working Paper 97-MWP 2, Center for Agriculture and Rural Development, Iowa State University, 1997.
[21] Ibid.

commodity from seed to food product will become a critical factor in agro-food trade. Genetically engineered seed with valuable output traits sought by particular end users will also require similar IP tracing and handing. This will mean the need to control the planting, tilling, harvesting, storage, processing, and distribution to target the end user willing to pay a premium over other similar products for the assurance of knowing where the product came from, how it was grown, and how it was processed.[22]

With IP production, producers and processors will need to better understand particular markets, e.g., seed, food, processing, or export, because each market may demand different characteristics. For example, a premium market in a distinctive variety of soybean for the Japanese tofu market requires that contract growers and handlers of these soybeans segregate their product to avoid any co-mingling with other soybeans. This means that an upstream grower must be able to provide documented assurances to the handler and processor that all the soybeans in a shipment contain the desired trait or do not contain other undesirable traits from the end users' perspective. Similarly, new European Union rules that set very strict limits on dioxin in food, feed, or feed material suggest that farmers may find IP production an increasingly necessary part of their marketing strategy. The recent StarLink episode, where a genetically engineered variety of corn not approved for human consumption found its way into food products, would have been much less likely to occur under a well-integrated agro-food value chain. The substantial costs of that co-mingling error underscore the rising importance of controlled production and tracing integrated through an agro-food value chain.

Grain attribute testing, tracking, and auditing systems organized by value-chains for new end uses are being established. These developments may create new opportunities for growth of specialized agricultural services and equipment. Rural areas could become sites of new business serving the needs of upstream value chain participants. For example, approximately 22% of grain elevators currently segregate genetically engineered corn and soybean varieties. Some elevators are now dedicating equipment and facilities to specific crops to avoid any chance of co-mingling with other varieties. Such practices may become as common for grain farmers as highly specified contracts have become for broiler production, suggesting the creation of extensive custom grain farming opportunities in the future.

---

[22] For example, field tests are currently underway for a genetically engineered corn variety that products gastric lipase enzyme useful in treating digestive disorders in cystic fibrosis sufferers.

ENVIRONMENTAL ISSUES IN
VALUE-ADDED PRODUCTION

Farms operating as part of a value chain may find that some form of environmental certification could become a significant value-added component of production. Agriculture is under intense pressures to improve its environmental performance. Environmental management systems (EMS) and associated eco-labeling or branding of products are becoming significant aspects of value-added production while EMSs are not new, they could take on significant greater importance in the futures as IP production gains market share. For over 20 years, Germany has had the *Umweltziechen* logo for products with positive environmental features; Japan has Eco Mark Program; Holland, the *Milieuker* logo to identify products as less environmentally damaging compared to most similar products; and the "Nordic Swan" label is the world's first multi-national eco-labeling scheme.[23] In addition to these eco-labels, there is an international organic certification system as well as dozens of regional organic certification programs in the U.S. Other labels denoting a product as produced by a particular EMS, e.g., integrated pest management, low-input, or "sustainable" are finding increased market visibility. Concerns about animal welfare are also likely to become reflected in IP systems.[24]

More recently, the International Organization for Standardization (ISO) introduced the ISO 14001 system to produce a set of standards for quality management to insure customer service. ISO 14001 is not an EMS *per se*, only the leading model for developing such a system. An EMS is a structured planning approach for a business to manage its environmental impacts; ISO 14001 is the "shell" in which a plan may be developed. It is also could provide a framework for addressing many aspects of quality assurance such as reducing food-borne illnesses or documenting how livestock are raised and slaughtered. Like its predecessor ISO 9000, ISO

---

[23] In 2002, Canada initiated two programs aimed at further developing environmentally responsible farming practices. Under the first program, eligible Canadian farmers will receive C$100 million over the next four years to help them implement environmental farm plans. The second program will make C$54.5 million available over six year to give Canadian producers better access to minor use and reduced-risk pesticides, thus helping increase their international competitiveness.

[24] U.S. supermarket and fast food industries introduced in 2002 the first comprehensive guidelines for the humane treatment of farm animals, recommending that farmers curtail such practices as starving hens to make them lay more eggs, housing pregnant pigs in crates so small they cannot fully lie down, and slaughtering some animals before they are fully unconscious.

14001 is increasingly viewed as a prerequisite for doing business in a global economy where assurances of quality, perceived or real, are becoming necessary business requirements. There are indications that agriculture is moving to embrace ISO 14001. Trade groups are actively pursuing quality assurance programs with EMS components. The American Soybean Association has joined other commodity groups such as the National Pork Council in developing such initiatives. Drawing on models used by Denmark and other countries, the Wisconsin Milk Marketing Board is also evaluating benefits of ISO 14001 certification.

INCREASED CONTRACT PRODUCTION

Agribusiness firms with control over proprietary product lines may come to rely exclusively on contract production and marketing in the future. Production of crops with particular output traits, e.g., traits affecting human food nutritional quality, may be done on a contract basis between a few individual farming operations and those owning or licensing the proprietary crop. A value chain integrator for a new line of tomato products, for example, could hold a license for a genetically engineered tomato variety with elevated levels of lycopene (an anti-cancer agent). The value chain integrator starts the IP process by contracting with particular farming operations that grow the tomato under highly controlled conditions, e.g., particular soils, watering schedules, growth inoculants, among others. The processor, in turn, must segregate the tomatoes and ship them along to canners or food processors who use the particular tomatoes in other value-added products which are then tested to verify their contents so that they may be labeled and sold at a premium. The market for these traits is not unlimited. The proprietary owners of the genetically engineered products are likely to require very specific growing, cultivating, harvesting, and processing conditions in order to assure the price premiums for these products. Such requirements make contracting with a few specially growers with custom farming operations a highly desirable arrangement for value chain integrators.[25]

Value chain developments could make some form of contract production a necessity for many producers. As integration of the agro-food

---

[25] Environmental management systems and the value of organic, eco-labeling, and other IP product development could also make "precision agriculture" in custom farming an increasingly important in value chain management. See CRS Report RL30630, *Precision Agriculture and Site-Specific Management: Current Status and Emerging Policy Issues.*

value chains deepens, however, fewer producers would be needed. Only those with contracts may find ready markets for their products. Because firms could find it costly and unwieldy to contract with many producers, those farmers and ranchers who become part of value chains may find that significant aspects of their status as independent commodity producers may become the price for being able to continue producing. As value chains expand, producers who sell undifferentiated commodities could find that today's spot markets for their commodities simply no longer exist. Producers might also bear greater risk in maintaining quality and delivery schedules in exchange for some pricing reliability and a ready market for their product. These characteristics exist today in the broiler industry and increasingly in the pork industry. They could diffuse globally to grains, soybeans, livestock, fruits, and vegetables in the not-too-distant future.

Not all producers welcome these changes. Some farmers and ranches are deeply concerned about the implications of these changes in production and marketing. Their concerns range from questioning about the viability of smaller family farms and highly integrated production and marketing systems to questions about the increased power that agro-food value chains cold have in shaping farmer and rancher options in the future. Anti-trust issues and related concerns over concentration in various agricultural sectors, e.g., livestock, have becoming increasingly important public policy issues over the past several years. Particular concerns have included the transparency of production contracts, the power of producers to contests terms in court, and the levels of market competition in some commodities.

Chapter 4

NEW VALUE-ADDED
AGRICULTURAL ENTERPRISES

Retaining locally produced capital and increasing the recirculation of money in local and regional economies are key development strategies. Value-added production is regarded by many observers as a way to keep more value of a commodity within a local economy and, thereby, stimulate economic growth and development. Much of the current discussion of value-added agriculture and rural development focuses on two general categories: (1) value-added food producers that offer or are perceived to offer higher quality, better nutrition, or greater convenience; and (2) industrial, non-food value-added products derived from grains, oil seeds, or non-traditional plants. These two general categories have potentially different implications for rural communities.

FOOD PROCESSING

Food processing is a very competitive, global business requiring constant product differentiation and innovation. High value-added food products that offer greater quality, or different nutritional factors, or increased convenience for consumers also tend to be labor intensive and to require more skilled workers, especially in product development and marketing. Value-added specialty food processing, however, uses relatively small quantities of agricultural prices or profitability. Small innovative firms may be particularly capable of developing this type of production of food produced through organic systems or regionally branded items are examples of enhanced economic value for which consumers are apparently willing to pay a premium over similar but undifferentiated products. Packing such products in microwaveable pouches, for example, could create further value based on the convenience of the product over traditionally processed frozen or canned products.

Available data on the local impact of value-added agricultural production tends to take existing commodity processing data and project the future importance of the sector to a state or regional economy. The example of Iowa discussed above is one of the better examples of this type of analysis. The operating lives of the more recently established facilities have probably not been long enough to draw valid conclusions; and there are relatively few examples of the socioeconomic impact of value-added production in the research literature. Some plants that began in the early 1990s are still operating and in some cases have expanded. For example, the American Italian Pasta Company has begun construction on a new pasta plant in Tolleson, Arizona, that initially will have an annual capacity of 100 million pounds, and later may be expanded to 200 to 300 million pounds. The company is the largest U.S. pasta producer and currently operates plants in Excelsior Springs, Missouri, Columbia, South Carolina, Kenosha, Wisconsin, and Verolanuova, Italy.

While this pasta plant expansion might be considered a positive outcome for many durum wheat producers, an important question is whether other areas can duplicate such success, especially rural areas.[1] These pasta plants are also located in or very near metro areas. Would a new farmer-owned pasta coop in rural Illinois be economically feasible? How much more demand exists for pasta in the next decade? It is the long-term picture that is most relevant to creating new rural development opportunities. A facility enjoying strong growth and profits today must eventually be able to survive on average growth and average profits. Whether that will happen or whether a single facility can survive is difficult to predict.

An important factor for sustained economic development, however, may be whether value-added agricultural facilitates can generate a regional economics of agglomeration or clustering of other facilities and supporting industries. The presence of a value-added agricultural plant that can attract other businesses would suggest a potentially much greater economic impact

---

[1] Congressional testimony in April, 2002 from a representative of the North American Millers Association revealed that while U.S. durum wheat farmers have outpaced domestic durum wheat demand in all but one of the last 10 years, they are, nonetheless, unable to produce the amount or quality of durum wheat demanded by U.S. pasta manufacturers. The result has been increased imports of Canadian durum wheat to supply this value-added market. *Sparks Policy Report*, April 24, 2002.

than a single plant. There is some evidence that this can happen. A wet million ethanol plant operated by Cargill in Eddyville, Iowa has attracted at least two additional plants that use output from the ethanol plant. One plant producers lysine which is used as an additive for animal feeds. The other plant manufacturers monosodium glutamate. Informal analysis has suggested that the three plants have provided economic stimulus to the Southeastern Iowa economy, mostly from the increased corn sales and the local multipliers from plant job. Similarly, the *Dakota Value Capture Cooperative* is planning a $65 million integrated beef, biogas generator, and ethanol complex north of Pierre, South Dakota that could create new opportunities in this predominantly farming region.

INDUSTRIAL VALUE-ADDED

Industrial value-added agricultural production uses a considerably larger volume of agricultural commodities than does value-added food production and may increase commodity prices over a wider area supplying agricultural manufacturing facilities. Value-added industrial production of agricultural commodities, however, tends to be capital intensive, and may employ fewer, and lower-skilled, workers relative to the investment needed or the value of the output. Corn-derived ethanol as a gasoline blending ingredient is one of the best known and most widely promoted example of an industrial value-added business, but a variety of other bio-based industrial products are also possible, e.g., starch, corn gluten, soy ink, bio-plastics.

New Bio-Based Products

In its 1987 report to then-Secretary of Agriculture, John Block, the New Farm and Forest Products Task Force recommended the development and commercialization of new agricultural products.[2] Their report called for a 25-year effort that would use 150 million acres of farmland, generate 750,000 jobs, increase farm income by $30 billion, and add $100 billion in national economic activity. The legislative result was the Alternative Agricultural Research and Commercialization Act of 1990 designed to assist the development and commercialization of new nonfood and nonfeed products derived from agricultural and forestry commodities. Under the 1996 farm

---

[2] The New Farm and Forest Products Task Force. *New Farm and Forest Products.*

bill (P.L. 106-627), AARC became a wholly owned government corporation. Preference was to be given to projects, which benefited rural communities and helped commercialize environmentally sound products. Table 11 lists examples of AARC projects.

Table 11. Selected AARC Projects, 1993

Project	Raw Material
Concentrated acid hydrolysis commercialization	Switchgrass or grain sorghum
Specialty fibers from Hesperaloe species	Hesperaloe (a new fiber crop)
Bio-plastic cotton	Cotton
Wheat gluten and wheat starch based adhesives, films, coatings, and food packing containers	Wheat
Newstone	Soybean flour and recycled newsprint
Kenaf/recycled fibers newsprint	Kenaf
Waste Pulp to Straw	Annual ryegrass straw
Ethanol based windshield washer solvent	Corn
Accelerated research and development of bio-diesel fuel	Soybeans and beef tallow
Bio-form, a concrete release agent	Rapeseed
Starch-encapsulated pest control formulations	Corn
Industrial coatings from soybeans oil	Soybeans

Source: U.S. Congress, Subcommittee on Rural Economy and Family Farming, Committee on Small Business, U.S. Senate, 103rd Congress, 1st Session, July 14, 1993.

Although the AARC was organized largely to develop innovative ways of using commodity surplus, it was essentially a value-added research and demonstration project oriented toward improving rural well-being. Authorization for the AARC, however, was repealed with the new farm bill (P.L. 107-171) and the program is currently closing out the remaining portfolio of projects. Because AARC projects were co-sponsored with private industry, some of the above projects are ongoing while others have ended. Primary data on local employment create by these projects or how these projects may have contributed to rural community development are unavailable. During FY2000 Appropriations hearings, however, the

Executive Director of the AARC testified that the AARC's return-on-investment was considerably ahead of its projected schedule after 7 years and that AARC-funded enterprises had produced an estimated 7,500 direct and indirect jobs in rural areas.[3]

Soybeans-derived products represent a large, well-established, and growing market. There are thousands of products on the market that contain soybeans. Rural areas in the Midwest may be well-positioned to participate in this sector of industrial value-added production, although one study concluded that a move to soybean-based ink by all the newspapers in the U.S. would result in, on average, only four new farming units per county for the Farm Belt states.[4] There may also be opportunity for farmer-owned value-added enterprises in new soybean processing operations. There is, however, little technological innovation within this mature sector. The industry is also currently dominated by large, well-established firms, e.g., Cargill.

Other industrial crops include *guayule*, a source of natural rubber, and *jojoba*, a desert shrub whose seed produces an oil used in cosmetics, ointments, and lubricants. Approximately 40,000 acres of *jojoba* were planted in the 1970s when a ban on sperm whale oil was initiated. While no estimate of jobs in *jojoba* processing are available, over 500 workers were estimated to be employed in the production of *jojoba* seed.[5] *Kenaf*, a reedy crop that grows 10-12 feet holds promise as a new source of insulation material for reducing road noise in cars and trucks.

ERS estimated the creation of about 40 new jobs from an estimated $10 million in sales for *crambe*, a contract-grown oil seed used for various industrial processes, especially plastics. *Crambe* was commercialized in the 1990s through the efforts of a team of farmers, agribusiness people, and scientists to develop a reliable domestic supply of erucic acid.[6] In 1990, North Dakota farmers teamed up with National Sun Industries (NSI) and North Dakota State University (NDSU) to produce about 2,200 acres of crambe, and within four years that team had nearly 59,000 acres of crambe under cultivation. NSI crushed the seed in their Enderlin, North Dakota, mill

[3] Statement of Robert E. Armstrong. Hearing before the Subcommittee on Agriculture, Rural Development, Food and Drug Administration, and Related Agencies, Committee on Appropriations, House of Representatives, March 17, 1999.

[4] Barkley, David L. and P.N. Wilson. "Is alternative agriculture a viable rural development strategy?" *Growth and Change*, 23, 2, 1992.

[5] Wilson, Paul. *"Nontraditional agriculture: an economic development alternative."* In David L. Barkley (ed) *Economic Adaptation: Alternatives for Non-Metropolitan Areas.* Westview Press, 1993.

[6] Erucic acid has an established market in erucamide, a preferred slip and antiblock agent for polyolefin films.

and marketed the oil and the co-product, defatted seed meal. Concurrently, the High Erucic Acid Development Effort (HEADE) team sponsored and conducted production breeding, processing, product development, and marketing research, including critical feeding experiments at NDSU that affirmed the efficacy of using crambe meal in cattle feed.[7]

In April 2002, Cargill and Dow Chemical opened a new $300 million bioplastics plant just outside Omaha, Nebraska, that will use up to 40,000 bushels daily of locally supplied corn as feedstock. The plant ferments corn starches to make lactic acid, whose molecules are then chained together to make biodegradable polymers, or plastic. The finished product resembles a ball the size of a marble or smaller that can be used by Cargill Dow customers to produce items ranging from the plastic film used on sleeves of golf balls or drinking cups to clothing, such as shirts, jackets and sweater. The plant is expected to employ about 100 workers hen it is at full capacity. Cargill and Dow will also be spending about $250 million over the next few years on commercial development, product technology development, and developments of technology to enable the conversion of biomass (such as corn stalks, wheat straw, grasses, and other agricultural waste products) to plastic. While no commercial applications are yet complete in the U.S., several are underway in Europe.

Researchers are also using advances in biotechnology to modify plants to produce industrial products and pharmaceuticals. Examples of products currently under development include: proteins and enzymes for diagnostic, therapeutic and manufacturing purposes; modified fatty acids and oils for paints and manufacturing; and specialty substances.[8] One potential research avenue currently being explored is using bacteria engineered to make polymers that closely resemble natural fibers. Biotechnology researchers are also developing ways to use biotechnology for environmental preservation and remediation. Other research is directed at enhancing plants' natural ability to absorb and store toxic and hazardous substances. Other promising biotechnology research includes using genetically modified plants to produce vaccines for human and animal illnesses ranging from colon cancer to diarrhea to tooth decay. Some of the plants used to develop vaccines include

---

[7] Kenneth D. Carlson, John C. Gardner, Vernon L. Anderson, and James J. Hanzel. "Crambe: New Crop Success." Pages 306-322. In: J. Janick (ed), *Progress in new crops*. ASHS Press, Alexandria, Va..1996.

[8] The Scripps Research Institute was granted a patent in July 2002, for a genetically modified corn plant that has been spliced a herpes-fighting human gene. Epicyte Pharmaceutical, which holds exclusive commercial rights to the patent, and its corporate partner, Dow Chemical Company, hope to extract the herpes-fighting antibody from the corn and turn it into a topical gel.

corn, spinach, tobacco, lettuce, tomato, soybeans and potatoes.[9] Charles Hurburgh, a specialist in grain quality at Iowa State University, predicts that 40% of the corn and soybeans grown in the United States will eventually contain a genetically engineered value-added trait for a specific end use, although it is by no means certain that these agronomic traits will necessarily create benefits of farmers. [10]

Energy from Biomass

The benefits of bioenergy were recognized in the Biomass Research and Development Act HR 2559 (Title III of the Agricultural Risk Protection Act of 2000, P.L. 106-224) and Executive Order 13134 (Developing and Promoting Biobased Industry and Bioenergy) which set the goal of tripling the use of biofuels and biobased products by 2010.[11] The NAS Report on Bio-Based Industry stated, "While there may be some potential for biobased industries to increase job opportunities, there are insufficient data to make accurate predictions of the impacts of biobased industries on future employment trends."[12] Assuming a multiplier based on the ration of sales to total employment in the chemical industries, the NAS researches estimated the creation of one million jobs. These would not be net jobs, however, inasmuch as current petrochemical jobs would be replaced.

Perhaps the most widely touted value-added enterprise is milling of wheat, barley, or corn for ethanol. Ethanol is the most visible product, but other by-products and co-products are also possible. Wet milling of corn for ethanol can also produce starches, corn-oil, amino acids, high-protein animal feeds, and commercial-grade carbon dioxide as valuable by-products or co-products of ethanol production. Farmer coops around the country have begun such projects to compete with ethanol, especially since California banned MTBE, the only commercially available gasoline oxygenate.[13] Farmer-owned coops have also gained market share in ethanol. A National Farmer's

---

[9] See *Harvest on the Horizon: Future Uses of Agricultural Biotechnology.* Report by the Pew Initiative on Food and Biotechnology, Washington, D.C., 2001.

[10] Hillyer, Gregg. "Biotech offers U.S. farmers promises and problems." *AgBioForum,* 2, 2, 1999; Coaldrake, Karen, "Trait enthusiasm does not guarantee on-farm profits." *AgBioForum,* 2, 2, 1999.

[11] See Ames, Jeremy and Carol Werner, "Revitalizing the Farm Economy via Renewable Energy Development," *BioCycle,* October, 2001.

[12] National Academy of Sciences. *Biobased Industrial Products: Research and Commercialization Priorities,* 2000.

[13] For a review of ethanol, see Yacobucci, Brent D. and Jasper Womach, *Fuel Ethanol: Background and Public Policy Issues.* CRS Report RL3069, February, 2002.

Union study recently showed that ADM and Cargill had only about 49% of the ethanol market, down from 67% in 1999. The Value-Added Development Act for American Agriculture (H.R. 1093), and the Farmers' Value-Added Agricultural Investment Tax Credit Act (H.R. 1094), both passed in the 107th Congress, would enhance the investment attractiveness of value-added ethanol plants. Other pending legislation would provide tax credit provisions specifically for ethanol production (S.907). Because of the current price disadvantages between ethanol and gasoline, tax subsidies are essential to ethanol production. Authorization for the current federal tax subsidy foe ethanol is scheduled to expire in 2008.

To estimate employment gains, the Renewable Fuels Association has used the figure of 3 plant workers for each million gallons of ethanol produced annually. Assuming a tripling by 2012 of the current 2 billion gallons annually of production capacity, that would mean approximately 18,000 new direct jobs in ethanol production by 2012. A 1997 report on ethanol production estimated the creation of nearly 200,000 direct and indirect jobs throughout the U.S. economy.[14] This outcome assumes the continuation of a federal tax subsidy for gasohol, a mixture of ethanol and gasoline. Several states as well have tax subsidies for gasohol (e.g., Wisconsin, Minnesota) that further contribute to the attractiveness of developing ethanol plants. Perhaps the biggest questions of ethanol production as a local development strategy is where the plants will locate and whether scale economies will favor a few large plants in a few communities or many small plants in many communities. A more recent study for the Renewable Fuels Association, for example, used a hypothetical 40 million gallon per year (MGY) plant to estimate regional activity and concluded that the impact would be significant (Box 3).

In addition to corn for ethanol production, other feedstocks may also be used. Waste products such as corn stover and other biomass may also become feedstocks for ethanol production. Whey from cheese making, for example, is the feedstock in a Wisconsin ethanol plant. Another Wisconsin company also plans to construct an ethanol plant at a dairy farm that will produce ethanol from cow manure. It will supply a high yield anaerobic digester technology that collects animal waste for fermentation. The

---

[14] Evans, Michael K. *The Economic Impact of the Demand for Ethanol*. Report prepared for the Midwestern Governor's Conference, February 1997.

maximum of methane or biogas collected is further processed in an alcohol conversion unit and distilled into different mixes of fuel grade ethanol.[15]

BOX 3. HYPOTHETICAL ECONOMIC IMPACT
OF FUTURE ETHANOL PLANTS

Results of a study found that building and operating a 40 MGY ethanol plant could:

- Provide a one-time boost of $142 million to the local economy during construction;
- Expand the local economic base by $110.2 million each year through direct spending of $52 million;
- Create 41 full-time plant jobs and 694 jobs throughout the entire economy;
- Increase local price of corn by 5-10 cents per bushel;
- Increase household income for the community by $19.6 million annually;
- Boost state and local sale tax receipts by an average pf $1.2 million depending on local rates;
- Provide an average of 13.3% annual return on investment over 10 years to a farmer investing over $20,000 in an ethanol facility.

Source: John Urbanchuk, AUS Consultant and Jeff Kapell of SJH & Company, *Ethanol and the Local Community*. Report for the Renewable Fuels Association, June 2002.

NEW VALUE-ADDED FARMING
AND MARKETING SYSTEMS

The traditional economic measure of bulk commodity production efficiency is the cost per unit of production, that is, yield per unit of capital. The lower the cost, the higher the production efficiency. With thin profit margins in bulk commodity production this has meant that ever larger-sized farms contributed to increased efficiencies as capital (in the form of

---

[15] The Internal Revenue Service approved a renewable energy production credit for 2002 of 1.8 cents per kilowatt-hour on the sale of electricity produced from wind energy, closed-loop biomass and poultry waste resources.

agricultural technology) substituted for labor. Value-added farming systems, however, may later that metric to income per acre, not yield per acre. Five acres of organic apples requiring intensive labor and selling for premium prices in the Japanese market may have equal or greater value than 25 acres of conventionally raised apples. Similarly, a smaller number of pasture-raised cattle, hogs, or poultry may command a higher price per pound than livestock raised in conventional feedlot and battery methods. Value-added farming systems producing products raised under alternative farming systems are able to command a premium price over other undifferentiated products. The organic market, for example, has been growing at approximately 20% for the past several years in the United States, Japan, and Europe.[16] While such rates may not be sustainable over the long-term, they do suggest a burgeoning market that value-added producers may target.[17]

Farmers markets, especially within urban areas, have grown significantly over the past 20 years, as consumers perceive locally grown produce as more desirable in a variety of ways. The number of farmers' markets in the Washington, D.C. area, for example, has increased dramatically over the past decade. Maryland saw an increase from 20 markets in 1990 to 72 in 2002.Virginia had 69 farmers markets in 2002, about eight more than in 2001. Washington has about 12 markets within the city limits. Locally grown, organic produce as become an important value-added product, especially for smaller producers in this market. While farmers markets account for only about 2% of total at-home food sale, supermarkets also have recognized the changing attitude of their consumers and have tried to compete by introducing more organic foods in their sales. Seventy percent of shoppers report their primary store sells natural or organic foods, according to the Food Marketing Institute. A survey of 1,000 adults for organic food company Walnut Acres conducted by Roper Starch Worldwide, found that 61% of consumers who buy organic products report that food safety is a major reason for doing so.[18] Such consumer demand for value-added products suggests that these markets may hold considerable

---

[16] The U.S. exported $40 million in organic products to the U.K. and $40-$60 million to Japan in 2000. Exports to the EU are growing at 15% annually; exports to Japan have grown between 30 and 50% a year between 1995-2000. When the United States fully implements its national organic standards in late 2002, exports of organic products could increase substantially. See Organic Trade Association, *Export Study for U.S. Organic Products to Asia and Europe*, 2001.

[17] The 2002 farm bill (P.L. 107-171) provides financial assistance to farmers who wish to get their operations certified as organic. The legislation also earmarks federal support ($15 million over five years) for research into organic production.

[18] Gardyn, Rebecca. "What's cooking?" *American Demographics.*, March, 2002.

opportunity for value-added producers in the future, especially of greater marketing support is provided. The 2002 farm bill, P.L. 107-171, for example, sets aside 15% (approximately $36 million from 2002 to 2007) of its value-added provision for support of organic marketing.

In Upstate New York, a Small Ruminant Meat Marketing project team at Cornell University has identified new ethnic markets that are not served by conventional producers. Halal slaughter and distribution facilities, live animal markets, Italian butcher shops, a gourmet processor and distributor, and a Kosher processor have each provided value-added opportunities to regional producers. Producers in other rural areas, especially those near major cities, many find similar value-added opportunities based on alternative production systems and niche markets (Box 4).

**BOX 4. ENTREPRENEURIAL OPPORTUNITIES
FOR SMALL SCALE PRODUCERS**

Several reports by universities and small farm advocacy groups participating in the USDA funded North Central Initiative for Small Farm Profitability offer hope to compete with low cost producers of major commodities but could find profitable niches and marketing avenues that offer new opportunities. Some of the examples apply only to farms close to metropolitan areas but others have general application. The initiative is a four state, multi-institutional effort designed to improve profitability and competitiveness of small and mid-sized farms through research, outreach and education. It brings together farmers, food and social scientists, marketers, extension educators and economists and others who attempt to identify, adapt and apply strategies that work. Coordinated by the University of Nebraska Center for Applied Rural Innovation, it also involves Iowa State, Missouri and Wisconsin land-grant universities, the center for Rural Affairs, Practical Farmers of Iowa and the Michael Fields Agricultural Institute, in Wisconsin. Eighteen case studies are profiled at http://www.farmprofitability.org/case.htm

---

Chapter 5

SUMMARY AND ASSESSMENT

The appeal of value-added agricultural production as a rural development strategy is not new. More than 60 years ago, Congress created the USDA Regional Utilization Centers to develop new products from agricultural commodities and to provide market-driven assistance to America's farmers.[1] In 1995, True D. Morse, President Eisenhower's Under Secretary for Agriculture, began the federal government's post-war rural development program with an investigation into the problems of low-income farmers and nonfarm rural populations.[2] Among his recommendations for improving rural welfare was creating new rural industries and improving the efficiency of industries processing and marketing farm products. Because many food-processing facilities were located near farming areas at that time, a major concern was increasing the supply of commodities, hence the need to improve local primary production, Marginal agricultural production dominated the poorest rural areas then. It was understandable that efforts to improve the efficiencies of that sector through farmer education, technical assistance, and extension, among other activities were desirable for paying a foundation for emerging manufacturing and industrial employment.

Today, however, there is no shortage of commodities. Food manufacturing facilities, with the exception of meat products manufacturing, grain processing, and some fruit and vegetable processing, are more likely to be located in metropolitan areas close to the consumer markets and to other

---

[1] Authorization for the four regional laboratories was provided in the Agricultural Adjustment Act of 1938. An important influence in the authorization was the chemurgy movement, especially the Chemurgy Council which was formed in 1935. "Chemurgy" refers to the development of new industrial products from organic raw materials, especially farm products.

[2] USDA. *Development of Agriculture's Human Resources*, 1995.

inputs rather than where raw material supplies exist. Also, the role of agriculture in most rural areas has declined. In only about a fifth of non-metro counties does agriculture account for 10% or more of labor and proprietor income today; and in only 312 of those counties does it rise to 20% or more. These counties are located predominantly in the Great Plains, Western Corn Belt, the Southeast, and Parts of the Northwest and are significant producers of bulk grains, soybeans, rice, and cotton, crops supported by federal farm payments. Although farm households have higher average incomes than non-farm households, manufacturing and service sector jobs now predominate in these counties. Rural manufacturing employment, while relatively high-waged, also tends to be lower skilled; and rural service sector employment is predominantly low-waged personal services. Counties where agriculture is significant are also likely to continue to decline in number as farms within these counties decline and the average size of the remaining ones increase. These 312 counties have also lagged behind other rural counties in creating new jobs in the 1990s. Little on the horizon suggests these general trends will jot continue into the future.

More recent legislation has attempted to broaden the opportunities for value-added agricultural enterprises as a strategy for rural development. The 1985 Farm Security Act (P.L. 99-198) contained provisions for entrepreneurial farm businesses and developing alternative fuels based on biomass. The Food, Agriculture, Conservation, and Trade Act of 1990 (P.L. 101-624) included provisions for Rural Technology Grants to assists the development and commercialization of new agricultural products and processes. The Federal Agricultural Improvement and Revitalization Act of 1996 (P.L. 106-127) also identified value-added agricultural processing as a target of Rural Cooperative Development Grants. The 2002 farm bill, the Farm Security and Rural Investment Act of 2002 (P.L. 107-171) makes value-added agriculture a major aspect of its rural development title. While individual successes can be identified, a review of the overall record of value-added agricultural enterprises as a significant generator of rural jobs, income, and community development suggests that such operations may become an important future source of stable rural employment and income in only a few areas. Most rural areas will need to look beyond agriculture and agricultural value-added production to crate new sources of competitive advantage.

The same may be said more specifically for food processing facilities. Many food producers do not use raw farm commodities as feedstocks but instead use semi-processed commodities, e.g., oil, meal, milk concentrates. These facilities also generally choose urban locations rather than rural areas to gain access to distribution networks and suppliers of other inputs. A recent USDA estimate concluded that if all urban food manufacturers suddenly relocated to rural areas, it would increase rural employment only by about 4%.[3] Bureau of Labor Statistics employment projections predict little job growth in the food processing sector, approximately 2% from 2002-2008, mostly in meat products manufacturing. This growth rate is significantly lower than the 14% growth rate projected for all industry from 2002-2008. Food processing, moreover, pays the lowest wages of all non-metro value-added industries; and hourly wages among production workers in meat product plants are the lowest of all food processing segments.

Food processing is also a fiercely competitive business, with the introduction of thousands of new products each year.[4] Only a third to a fifth of these products survive in the market for any length of time.[5] Food processing enterprises may be more labor intensive than, for example, ethanol plants or soybean processing facilities, but the likelihood that small food processors can successfully compete with better capitalized, globally competitive food processors, and survive over the short term, does not seem high. Over 77% of new food products are duplicates of the same product by a different manufacturer with only about 15% considered "classically innovative." Six percent of new food introductions are simply line extensions, e.g., a different size container.[6]

While small-to-medium sized firms introduced approximately 86% of new food products, half of all food processing establishments employ 20 or fewer workers. Were a small processing facility to achieve a degree of economic success, it could be acquired by a larger food processing and marketing company. Were the existing facility to be expanded at its original site, employment might be sustained and perhaps increased. But, an acquiring firm may as likely decide to move production to an existing facility closer to consumer markets, i.e., metropolitan areas. A small-scale food processing operation relying on seasonal products, e.g., fruits, and part-time labor, may offer some degree of expanded income opportunities, but as sources of sustained rural employment and development, such enterprises are unlikely to weather the mid-term. If such firms share the fate of the majority

---

[3] Gale, Fred and Maureen Kilkenny. "Agriculture's role shrinks as the service economy expands." *Rural Conditions and Trends.*" Vol. 10, 2, July 2000.

[4] New food products in the United States increased to nearly 17,000 in 1995, but declined to slightly over 9,000 by 2000. See J. Michael Harris, "Food product introductions continue to decline in 2000." *FoodReview,* 25, 1, Spring, 2002.

[5] Ibid.

[6] Ibid.

of small start-up businesses, most new small food processing operations are unlikely to have even 5-year survival rates.

The total number of farms and the share of agriculture-related income in the rural economy continue to decline. Most agricultural value-added enterprises, while not unimportant to income gains for particular farm households, seem unlikely to provide the basis for substantive development of related or supportive businesses in rural areas. The larger, more capital-intensive manufacturing enterprises, e.g., ethanol production or soybean processing, do not provide large numbers of jobs nor do they seem likely to generate significant growth of other businesses. If the enterprise is owned by a new-generation agricultural cooperative, whose members also own supply contracts, their markets for bulk commodities may be enhanced. The local economic picture may be different if, on the other hand, the enterprise is owned by external investor, e.g., large corporations like Archer Daniels Midland or Cargill, which currently dominate ethanol and soybean processing and distribution. Even with expanded market share from farmer cooperatives, however, ethanol, corn starch, soy oil, soy meal, and other semi-processed goods are essentially undifferentiated, bulk commodities made form undifferentiated, bulk commodities.

Farmer cooperatives that supply and/or own smaller-scale, custom meat processing and packing facilities may provide new opportunities for some ranchers. Pastured-livestock raising and hormone/antibiotic-free animal production systems are increasingly sought by consumers here and abroad, as the negative effects of highly industrialized production become more widely perceived. The same is true for eggs and value-added egg products, whole milk, and dairy products. These products may present possibilities for value-added entrepreneurs through regional branding or direct marketing, e.g., farmers markets or Community Supported Agricultural programs.[7] Custom meat packing and dairy facilities to serve these markets have potential to improve the incomes of producers, especially those developing new marketing channels within metro areas. But here, as well, the question arises whether incremental income improvements for some farm households can be translated into more generalized economic growth and regional development where most residents currently have little or nothing to do with the agricultural production sector.

Communities that become supply chain hubs through supporting a meat packing and processing facility or bulk commodity processor may become

---

[7] Community Supported Agriculture programs involve local residents or local organizations contracting with local producers for a share of a producer's farm output.

regional centers for value-added agricultural jobs. Incomes provided by these facilities can have a positive impact on the local and regional economy. Some rural areas that have sought to become large industrial agricultural production sites, however, have found that the cost of creating such jobs can be greater than the value of the income stream from the jobs.[8] Growth in transportation and storage-related employment could accompany an agricultural supply chain hub. Whether such enterprises might also generate net jobs in other agriculturally related businesses and services is unknown. Related business support services could find that locating near such facilities is desirable. On the other hand, the location of business support services could continue its trend toward metropolitan locations.

New specialty crops and organic production each suggest some positive income benefit to individual growers who can develop new products and successfully service niche markets and, in time, grow niches into larger markets. Federal support for these alternative crop and farming systems could help make agricultural enterprises more viable in some areas. Manufacturing facilities for extracting new bioengineered plant or animal products may also become a future growth area. Such operations, to the extent that they require new types of agriculture-related labor skills, could increase job opportunities for some local residents, although the extend to which such operations might become substantive sources of rural growth is entirely speculative. If production capital and income from these operations circulate largely within the local area, the local profit picture can improve. If production occurs under supply contracts where the contractor provides most of the inputs, however, less capital may circulate locally. Value-added agricultural operations located within metro regions or within commuting distance to metro areas could benefit from these markets. Farms located in such areas, however, are also more likely to be within more diversified economies and to generate jobs and income that contribute only a small share of the rural economy. In more remote rural areas, the Internet may offer marketing possibilities to some producers. The employment and income-generating aspects of such operations though, do not suggest they will become significant sources of rural development.

The logic of supply/value chains opens he potential for small-scale value-added producers to achieve more competitive scale economies by connecting small-scale processors or niche market producer to equally small-scale IP raw material producers. For example, organic fruit producer

---

[8] North Central Regional Center for Rural Development. *Bringing Home the Bacon: The Myth of the Role of Corporate Hog Farming in Rural Revitalization.* Report to the Kerr Center for Sustainable Agriculture. 1999.

cooperatives and IP bulk commodity producers, e.g., non-genetically engineered corn and soybeans, or hormone-free beef, might supply branded food processors with raw materials. With the market for both organic and convenient foods growing, large food processors are likely to want stable, consistent supplies of IP commodities for their production. Agricultural cooperatives engaged in organic or "environmentally friendly" production techniques, especially those near urban and suburban consumers, might also supply regional markets, including retail outlets such as restaurants and grocery outlets.

   Consistency and reliability in supply and quality of products are significant hurdles for any value-added producer. Agro-food value chains are designed to increase such consistency and reliability. New generation cooperatives that can develop and manage the links in a value chain may benefit from this emerging development in the organization for production. Modification and improvement to local and regional transportation infrastructure to complement value chain agriculture may also become necessary. Existing rail and water infrastructure, for example, is based largely on the requirements of traditional agriculture, that is, the movements of undifferentiated bulk grains to market. Small-scale niche producers may require new technologies that can better support IP shipping and handling.[9] Entrepreneurs able to master the links along the value chain could create new opportunities for themselves as well as creating a viable agricultural sector within a more diversified regional economy.

   From a policy perspective, it is perhaps helpful to distinguish between value-added and non-traditional agricultural production as potentially useful business management strategies, risk diversification tools, or enhanced income sources, and value-added agricultural production as a more general rural economic development strategy. Low labor costs and access to raw commodities in rural areas will continue to be attractive to some value-added processors. For some farmers in some locations, capturing more value in their farm crop through an ethanol plant or from their durum wheat through a pasta plant can also make important contributions to household income and provide opportunities for new manufacturing employment in rural areas. Investing in alternative production systems such as organic agriculture, or intensively-grazed livestock, or developing new markets for regionally branded products might also contribute to maintaining agriculture in some

---

[9] Robert Heuer. "Where's agriculture's transportation agenda?" *Ag Lender Magazine*, April, 2001.

areas or on farms that are not able to compete on the industrial logic of ever-lower unit production costs.

Job diversification in many areas dominated by agriculture is limited. Most rural areas are increasingly tied to urban, suburban, and global systems in complex ways that steadily shrink agriculture's role in the rural economy relative to other sectors. Agriculture is becoming a more technologically sophisticated and knowledge-based industry with closer ties to metropolitan areas. Some job seekers and entrepreneurs may find rural value-added agricultural production attractive for other than monetary reasons, e.g., living in a rural area. But most rural job seekers will continue to find areas with more diversified economies will be better positioned to develop new growth opportunities in the future.

Agriculture, however, will remain an important if diminished part of many rural economies. Value-added agriculture can very likely improve local opportunities in some areas where non-farm jobs are scarce or nonexistent. Where viable local opportunities can be identified and developed, they should probably be encouraged and supported. Enhanced federal investment in research and demonstration could be targeted to better ensure that farmers, entrepreneurs, and rural communities are well-positioned to benefit from value-added production and new uses from new crops. Efforts to support smaller-scale farming opportunities can also contribute to the overall stability of many rural economies. But as a new engine of rural development in the sense of creating a significant source of stable, well-paying local jobs, generating the basis for expanded local and regional development, and improving the general welfare of most rural citizens and rural communities, value-added agriculture production shows promise in comparatively few places.

Value-added agriculture as a significant programmatic vehicle for rural development suffers from the fundamental weakness of viewing rural policy issues largely through the lens of agriculture, and more specifically, through farming. With over 90% of today's rural population unconnected to farming and with most income for most farm households originating in off-farm sources, farming or new agriculturally-related businesses appear unlikely to stem the trend of declining employment opportunities in many rural areas, especially remote, farming-dependent counties. Traditional farming and modern agribusiness increasingly consist of two separate socioeconomic enterprises, the former connected closely to place, the latter increasingly independent of any particular location. While it is substantially true that agriculture will remain an important factor in many regional economies, what benefits farm-household income alone no longer addresses the many issues facing rural America as a whole. Renewed efforts to build on rural America's old competitive advantages in agriculture and low-skilled manufacturing, rather than creating new competitive advantages in emerging sectors, is likely to be a marginal strategy at best for sustaining most rural areas over the long-term.

INDEX

F

farm families, 20
farm households, 3, 7, 20, 48, 50, 53
farm structure, 26
farmers, vii, 14, 22, 30, 31, 33, 36,
    39, 41, 44, 45, 47, 50, 52, 53
farming, vii, 2-6, 11, 20-22, 24, 27,
    30-32, 37, 39, 44, 47, 51, 53
farming dependent, 11
fatty acids, 40
federal government, 47
fiber system, 20, 26
fishing, 18

G

grains, 2, 28, 29, 33, 35, 48, 52
grants, 5, 6, 10
Great Plains, 10, 20, 21, 27, 48

H

High Erucic Acid Development
    Effort (HEADE), 40
household income, 5, 7, 17, 20, 43,
    52
households, 13, 48
housing, 14, 31
human capital, 14

I

identity preserved (IP), vii, 1, 2, 4,
    28, 30-32, 52
immigrants, 11
immigration, 10, 11, 14
industrial, 1, 3, 4, 10, 24, 35, 37, 39,
    40, 47, 51, 53
intellectual property rights, 6
International Organization for
    Standardization (ISO), 31

J

job growth, 13, 15, 49
job seekers, 24, 53
joint ventures, 26

L

labor markets, 10-12
large family farms, 27
limited-resource, 14
loans, 10
local residents, 51
low-input, 31

M

manufacturing, 1, 2, 4, 8, 11, 12, 14,
    15, 18-20, 22, 24, 25, 37, 40, 47,
    49, 50, 52, 54
manufacturing jobs, 12, 13, 24
manufacturing purposes, 40
manufacturing sector, 19, 20, 24
marketing system, 2, 33
metro regions, 19, 51
metropolitan areas, 4, 11, 45, 47, 49,
    53
Metropolitan Statistical Area (MSA),
    10
migration, 10, 11
milk, 48, 50
million gallon per year (MGY), 42,
    43
mining, 8, 23
Mississippi Delta, 10

N

National Sun Industries (NSI), 39
non-food value-added products, 35
non-metro areas, 9, 11, 15, 17, 19-22
non-metro counties, 8, 10, 11, 48